ANIMALS AND PLANTS

Adam Rapp

BROADWAY PLAY PUBLISHING INC
New York
www.broadwayplaypublishing.com
info@broadwayplaypublishing.com

ANIMALS AND PLANTS
© Copyright 2002 by Adam Rapp

All rights reserved. This work is fully protected under the copyright laws of the United States of America. No part of this publication may be photocopied, reproduced, stored in a retrieval system, or transmitted, in any form or by any means, electronic, mechanical, recording, or otherwise, without the prior permission of the publisher. Additional copies of this play are available from the publisher.

Written permission is required for live performance of any sort. This includes readings, cuttings, scenes, and excerpts. For amateur and stock performances, please contact Broadway Play Publishing Inc. For all other rights contact the author c/o B P P I.

1st printing: May 2006

I S B N: 978-0-88145-312-6

ANIMALS AND PLANTS was first published by B P P I in May 2002 in *Plays by Adam Rapp*.

Book design: Marie Donovan
Word processing: Microsoft Word
Typographic controls: Ventura Publisher
Typeface: Palatino
Printed and bound in the U S A

ANIMALS AND PLANTS premiered at the American Repertory Theater (Robert Brustein, Artistic Director) on 30 March 2001 with the following cast and creative contributors:

BURRIS . . . . Benjamin Evett
DANTLY . . . . Will LeBow
CASSANDRA . . . . Frances Chewning
A MAN . . . . Scott A Albert
WEATHER REPORTER ON T V . . . . Karen MacDonald

Director . . . . Scott Zigler
Set . . . . J Michael Griggs
Costumes . . . . Jane Alois Stein
Lighting . . . . John Ambrosone
Sound . . . . .David Remedios
Stage manager . . . . .M Pat Hodge
Production dramaturg . . . . Gideon Lester

CHARACTERS & SETTING

BURRIS
DANTLY
CASSANDRA
A MAN

Setting: a small motel room

Place: Boone, North Carolina

Time: the middle of a snowstorm

ACT ONE

(A cheap motel room. There is a single, king-sized bed, simple furnishings. DANTLY, *mid-thirties and rather large, is on top of the covers, watching the T V, his hand down his pants. Barely audible, the newscast from the T V reports a terrible snowstorm. The curtains have been pulled aside and the blinds are open. Snow is diagonal in the window, its volume unbelievable.* BURRIS, *younger and smaller, perhaps thirty and very crafty, is standing in front of the window, eating beef jerky. He wears a white T-shirt and boxer shorts. He is staring out into the night.)*

BURRIS: Wow.

DANTLY: Wow what.

BURRIS: There's like this thing that happens.

DANTLY: What thing?

BURRIS: When you watch it.

DANTLY: Watch what?

BURRIS: The fucking snow, man. If you stare into it. Something like starts to take shape. It sort of has limbs.

DANTLY: Like from a tree?

BURRIS: Like from a man.

DANTLY: Maybe it's him.

BURRIS: Maybe.

DANTLY: It's about time.

BURRIS: I know, right?

DANTLY: Seven hours late.

BURRIS: Seven fucking hours, man. Zankich sends us out in a goddamn blizzard. I'm skitzed. You're all hypnotized from driving. How's your dick?

DANTLY: Still hurts.

BURRIS: Did it stop bleeding?

DANTLY: I think so.

BURRIS: I don't know what possessed you to put that ice scraper down your pants.

DANTLY: I don't wanna talk about it.

(Pause)

BURRIS: Fucking Zankich. Ordering us around like we're his minions. You notice how his voice has changed lately? His tone or whatever? ...We're like all snowbound while he watches pay-per-view in his high-rise pussy pad. He's prolly got vadge on the sofa as we speak.

DANTLY: You think?

BURRIS: Oh, totally, Dantly. I'll bet he's sporting some surgically enhanced European chick he picked up on Fifth Avenue. Some German airport whore with bionic tits and expensive sunglasses. I can just see it: coke all over the coffee table, sun tan lotion soaking into the furniture. My gonads are shrinking just thinking about it. Motherfucking Zankich. I'm tired of leaving the city broke, man. Next time he's got a job for us I'm asking for half up front. It's fucking larceny.

DANTLY: ...Um, Burris?

BURRIS: Huh.

DANTLY: What are minions?

ACT ONE

BURRIS: Underlings, man. Underlings or like subordinates or whatever. *(He stares out the window.)*

DANTLY: He still there?

BURRIS: No.

DANTLY: It's like that thing that happens in the desert.

BURRIS: What, sand?

DANTLY: No, that other thing.

BURRIS: A mirage?

DANTLY: Yeah, a mirage.

(Pause)

DANTLY: Wanna do state capitals?

BURRIS: I'm tired of doing state capitals.

DANTLY: Okay.

(Pause)

DANTLY: What's the capital of Idaho?

BURRIS: Idahoville.

(Pause)

DANTLY: What did Zankich say this guy would look like, anyway?

BURRIS: He didn't say. He just called him The Burning Man. He said we'd know who he was when we saw him.

DANTLY: The Burning Man. Weird.

BURRIS: Oh, it's totally weird.

DANTLY: Do you think that's his real name?

BURRIS: I doubt it.

DANTLY: It's sorta cool.

BURRIS: The Burning Man. A man aflame.

DANTLY: Maybe he's like on fire.

BURRIS: Maybe.

DANTLY: Like his hair. His hair or his...what are they called?

BURRIS: Sideburns.

DANTLY: Yeah, or like his sideburns.

BURRIS: The Fucking Burning Man, man.

DANTLY: He like burns.

BURRIS: Enter the Burning Man. Flight of the Burning Man. The Falcon and the Burning Man.

DANTLY: Breakfast with the Burning Man.

BURRIS: Breakfast with the Burning Man! I'll bet he's a tall fucker.

DANTLY: You think?

BURRIS: Yeah, for some reason I see him as like six-six and really skinny.

DANTLY: Really skinny, huh?

BURRIS: Like six-six-and-a-half, one thirty-five.

DANTLY: Whoa.

BURRIS: Like that freak Zankich brought back from Sarajevo.

DANTLY: Dragon?

BURRIS: Yeah, Dragon. The child molester.

DANTLY: Zankich said he's really good at basketball. Like he played on some team for a while.

BURRIS: Yeah?

DANTLY: Yeah. He got like drafted and everything.

BURRIS: Good for him.

ACT ONE

DANTLY: That's pretty cool, right?

BURRIS: Oh, it's just enormously unbelievable. Fucking Europeans.

(*Pause*)

DANTLY: I'm thinkin about changin my name.

BURRIS: Really.

DANTLY: Uh-huh.

BURRIS: Changing it to what?

DANTLY: I don't know. Maybe like Dave.

BURRIS: Like Burning Dave?

DANTLY: No. Just Dave.

BURRIS: What's wrong with Walt?

DANTLY: I don't know.

BURRIS: Dude, Walt Dantly has a good rhythm to it.

DANTLY: It does?

BURRIS: Oh, totally. It's better than Dan Burris.

DANTLY: You think?

BURRIS: Dan Burris the fucking family man. Dan Burris the guy with three-point four kids and the gabled garage. I like your name. It's a pitcher's name.

DANTLY: It is?

BURRIS: Yeah, man. Walt Dantly. I see a guy with this totally unhittable fastball. Good changeup. Pinpoint control. A lefty.

DANTLY: I'm not a lefty.

BURRIS: I know. But it's still a cool name. When I hear Dan Burris I see this like fleshy-looking newscaster. Some totally tan dick with pancake batter on his face.

Walt Dantly is so much cooler. It even sounds a little French.

DANTLY: It does?

BURRIS: *I* think so.

DANTLY: Huh.

(Pause)

BURRIS: So what like prompted this idea about changing your name?

DANTLY: I guess I'm startin to see myself as different.

BURRIS: Different from what?

DANTLY: From what I am now.

BURRIS: Well, what are you now, exactly?

DANTLY: Um. I don't know, Burris. What do you think I am now?

*(*BURRIS *thinks.)*

DANTLY: See? I'm like this blank.

BURRIS: You're not blank.

DANTLY: Yes I am. I mean, outside of workin for Zankich what do I do?

BURRIS: You do stuff.

DANTLY: I don't, though. I sit around. I watch T V.

BURRIS: You do more than that.

DANTLY: No I don't.

BURRIS: Sure you do.

DANTLY: Like what?

BURRIS: You go to the zoo.

DANTLY: Not anymore.

BURRIS: You used to go all the time.

ACT ONE

DANTLY: I haven't been to the zoo in years.

BURRIS: So you think changing your name to Dave is gonna help?

DANTLY: I think it will, yes.

BURRIS: So what would *Dave* Dantly be?

DANTLY: I don't know. Somethin, though. Maybe like a chef.

BURRIS: A chef.

DANTLY: Yeah, a chef.

BURRIS: Like with a big white hat?

DANTLY: Sure, why not?

BURRIS: And those dickish pants they wear?

DANTLY: Those pants aren't dickish.

BURRIS: Dude, they're totally dickish.

DANTLY: Girls like those pants.

(Pause)

BURRIS: A chef, huh? I could see that.

DANTLY: I could like make salads. Tomatoes and lettuce and stuff. The dressings. The people in the kitchen could call me Double D.

BURRIS: Double D. I like that.

DANTLY: See?

(Pause)

BURRIS: I used to know this chef. He died.

DANTLY: How did he die?

BURRIS: Nose cancer.

DANTLY: Whoa.

BURRIS: Yeah, eventually his whole face fell off.

(Pause)

DANTLY: Hey, Burris, what's a gable?

BURRIS: It's like a roof crotch.

DANTLY: What the fuck is a roof crotch?

BURRIS: That place where snow settles. Like where it gets heaped or whatever.

DANTLY: Oh. I think I had one of those once.

(The phone rings. DANTLY *answers it.)*

DANTLY: Hello? ...Hello? *(He sets the phone down.)*

BURRIS: Who was it?

DANTLY: I don't know.

BURRIS: Why not?

DANTLY: There was no voice.

BURRIS: There was no fucking voice?

DANTLY: Nu-uh. Just breathing.

BURRIS: Like heavy breathing?

DANTLY: Like breathing when-somebody's-sleeping breathing.

BURRIS: Weird.

DANTLY: I know, right?

BURRIS: Maybe it's that chick from the head shop. You gave her our number, right?

DANTLY: Yeah, I gave it to her.

BURRIS: She was hot, man.

DANTLY: She was okay.

BURRIS: No, Dantly, she was fucking hot. She was like hot hot.

DANTLY: You think?

ACT ONE

BURRIS: Yeah, man. Like in that arty way.

DANTLY: You thought she was arty?

BURRIS: Totally.

DANTLY: Like arts and crafts arty?

BURRIS: Like Birkenstock-and-lanyard arty. Like underarm hair arty.

DANTLY: Really?

BURRIS: She was totally crunchy.

DANTLY: Like big bush crunchy?

BURRIS: Like Chewbacka bush crunchy.

DANTLY: Saskwatch crunchy.

BURRIS: Fucking Saskwatch crunchy, man!

(Pause)

DANTLY: What's a lanyard anyway?

BURRIS: It's one of those little braided leashes.

DANTLY: Like a dog leash?

BURRIS: No, like a wrist leash. For keys or whatever. Whistles.

DANTLY: Oh.

(BURRIS *crosses to his bag, removes a pair of hand strengtheners, squeezes them while staring in the mirror.*)

DANTLY: So you think she was interested?

BURRIS: She was totally checking you out, man.

DANTLY: Bullshit.

BURRIS: Her eyes were all over you, Dantly. She was like optically feasting on your ass.

DANTLY: Huh... You think that was her on the phone?

BURRIS: Maybe.

DANTLY: Maybe she'll call back.

BURRIS: I'll bet she does.

DANTLY: I should prolly shower at some point.

BURRIS: I would.

DANTLY: I've been farting a lot.

BURRIS: It's all the pizza. The pizza and the beer.

DANTLY: I'm thinking about becoming a vegetarian. It's supposed to be good for your insides. Your like organs or whatever.

(BURRIS *starts to eat the last piece of beef jerky, sits next to* DANTLY *on the bed, bounces around, comes to rest with his back against the headboard. They watch T V.*)

BURRIS: Huh.

DANTLY: Yeah, they're filming snow.

BURRIS: The weather chick is hot. It's like she has a secret. Man, I love that: a chick with a secret.

DANTLY: A chick with a secret.

BURRIS: Like she used to be a tennis pro. Or like she knows karate.

DANTLY: Karate's cool. The robe. The bowing.

BURRIS: She could totally fuck you up, man. Like you'd be all touchy-feely and then—*WHAM, SISTER!* (*He explodes with some black belt theater, returns to stillness.*) I like how she's almost black.

DANTLY: Yeah, is that a tan or what?

BURRIS: Maybe. She might be Indian.

DANTLY: Like Indian-from-India Indian?

BURRIS: Like Native American.

DANTLY: She should have a feather.

ACT ONE

BURRIS: Or like a hatchet.

DANTLY: Tiger Lilly.

BURRIS: I love Tiger Lilly.

DANTLY: She used to give me a boner.

BURRIS: Peter Pan fucked up.

DANTLY: Wendy was so uptight, right?

BURRIS: Yeah, man. Fuck Wendy. Tiger Lilly all the way.

(They watch.)

DANTLY: Burris?

BURRIS: Yeah, Dantly?

DANTLY: Why are there like no black people in my life?

BURRIS: What do you mean?

DANTLY: I mean, I live in New York City and there are no black people in my life.

BURRIS: So?

DANTLY: So, I used to know what it was to be black. Like how to talk. The words they use or whatever.

BURRIS: Culture changes.

DANTLY: For instance, the night before we did that job for Zankich down in Sarasota, I walked into this church on a Hundred and Fourteenth Street. There was a gospel choir. Whole drum kit set up right on the altar. I was the only white person. They sing with their whole bodies. They lean into it. Like there's a higher purpose or whatever.

I sang too, Burris. I sang so hard my throat got sore. I didn't even know the words, but I let it rip for like forty-five minutes.

And when it was over I just sat there. In like the pews or whatever. I sat there and I stared at Jesus. Their Jesus is black, Burris. And not like painted black. He's like one of those brothers you see walkin across Saint Nicholas Avenue in red leather.

BURRIS: Like Feuce from Brownsville.

DANTLY: Yeah, exactly. Like Feuce from Brownsville. But without the dreads.

BURRIS: He told me he keeps weed in his dreads.

DANTLY: Really.

BURRIS: Yeah, like these big stinky buds. That's how he deals it.

DANTLY: He pulls it out of his hair?

BURRIS: Oh totally, man. He let me smell it.

DANTLY: That's so cool.

(BURRIS *crosses to his bag, removes a chest cord, starts to flex it in front of the mirror.*)

DANTLY: It was weird.

BURRIS: What was weird?

DANTLY: Sitting alone in that church I felt smaller than ever. Even further away.

BURRIS: Further away from what?

DANTLY: I don't know, Burris. Like Heaven maybe.

(*Pause*)

DANTLY: Yeah, I used to have some black in me. I had certain shoes and hats. There was something in my walk. Now I'm just this white guy.

BURRIS: People change. It's in our nature.

DANTLY: I'm going through this phase where I'm puttin things down my pants.

BURRIS: Yeah, like fucking ice scrapers.

ACT ONE

DANTLY: Ice scrapers. Silverware. Jars of peanut butter.

BURRIS: You put jars of peanut butter down your pants?

DANTLY: Uh-huh.

BURRIS: Why.

DANTLY: I don't know. I guess it makes me feel like I'm getting away with somethin.

(BURRIS *finishes with the chest chord.*)

BURRIS: Hey, Dantly, why the fuck did you walk into that church on a Hundred and Fourteenth Street?

DANTLY: I don't know. Cause I was lonely I guess. I thought it would make me feel like connected or whatever.

BURRIS: You should've called me. You could've come over, shot the shit, played some cards.

DANTLY: Yeah?

BURRIS: Of course, man. You're welcome any time. How long we been partners?

DANTLY: A while, right?

BURRIS: Ten years, man. That's a fucking decade. You spend a decade with someone and you earn certain inalienable rights.

DANTLY: Thanks, Burris.

(BURRIS *stares out the window.*)

DANTLY: Is the car totally buried?

BURRIS: Totally buried.

DANTLY: We'll have to dig it out eventually.

BURRIS: Eventually we will.

DANTLY: I wonder what would happen if you just like went into it.

BURRIS: What, the car?

DANTLY: No, the snow.

BURRIS: What do you mean?

DANTLY: Like if you opened the door and just started walking.

BURRIS: With like snowshoes?

DANTLY: No snowshoes.

BURRIS: A coat?

DANTLY: No coat.

BURRIS: What about earmuffs? You gotta at least throw in a pair of earmuffs, man.

DANTLY: No clothes. No nothing.

BURRIS: You mean like forge out into the blizzard naked?

DANTLY: Yeah. You'd just like strip and open the door and start walking. I wonder what would happen?

BURRIS: You'd fucking die is what would happen. You'd get hypothermia.

DANTLY: You think?

BURRIS: You'd be okay for about fifteen minutes or so and then you'd probably start like slipping around in these totally panic-stricken circles and collapse under a birch tree, get frostbite, fucking freeze to death.

DANTLY: I don't know, Burris.

BURRIS: What do you mean you don't know? Fifteen minutes, man. Twenty minutes tops.

DANTLY: Maybe things would get like really quiet or something. Maybe it wouldn't be cold at all.

BURRIS: I think you need some sleep, Walt.

ACT ONE

(Pause)

DANTLY: Hey Burris, did you bring any jock itch spray?

BURRIS: Um. No.

DANTLY: Oh.

BURRIS: I don't have jock itch.

DANTLY: You don't?

BURRIS: No.

DANTLY: Then what's that stuff you're always spraying on your balls?

BURRIS: Right Guard.

DANTLY: You spray Right Guard on your balls?

BURRIS: Yeah, man. I like to keep things fresh down low. Why, do you have jock itch?

DANTLY: I'm not sure.

BURRIS: Well, does it itch and burn?

DANTLY: Not really.

BURRIS: Is it like scaly or moltish?

DANTLY: Um, no.

BURRIS: Well, what makes you think you have jock itch?

DANTLY: I don't know. Maybe I'd just like to try your Right Guard.

BURRIS: On your balls?

DANTLY: Yeah, you always look so relieved when you're finished... Does that feel good?

BURRIS: I like it.

DANTLY: Maybe I'll try it later.

BURRIS: Okay.

DANTLY: What's moltish?

BURRIS: It's what birds do. They molt. It has to do with feathers.

DANTLY: Oh.

(BURRIS *does some kung fu the mirror.*)

BURRIS: Yeah, I like being a man. How bout it, right?

DANTLY: Sure.

BURRIS: I wouldn't want it any other way. I mean we travel. We have a gun. We have a bag of cash. We're beyond a certain age and we're these total like guys. It gives me great satisfaction.

DANTLY: ...I shaved my ass today.

BURRIS: You did?

DANTLY: Yeah.

BURRIS: When?

DANTLY: When you went out looking for a snow shovel. I went into the bathroom and shaved it.

BURRIS: Like the whole thing?

DANTLY: Uh-huh.

BURRIS: Both cheeks?

DANTLY: Both cheeks.

BURRIS: The crack and everything?

DANTLY: No, I left the crack alone.

BURRIS: Wow. So now you have these like totally slick buns.

DANTLY: I do.

BURRIS: How does it feel?

DANTLY: I like it.

BURRIS: Cool. You could be like this total bobsledder. Or a lugist. Does it itch?

DANTLY: Not really.

BURRIS: Cause I got some shaving lotion.

DANTLY: No thanks.

BURRIS: Well, if it starts itching, just let me know. It's Old Spice.

DANTLY: It was weird, Dan. When I was shaving my ass I had the feeling that someone was watchin me. I kept wantin to check behind the shower curtain.

BURRIS: So you're a little paranoid. It was a long drive. All that snow hitting the windshield. It was fucking relentless. You need a break, man.

DANTLY: Maybe.

(Pause)

BURRIS: So, um, why'd you shave your ass, Walt?

DANTLY: I don't know. I did it after my tooth fell out.

BURRIS: Your fucking tooth fell out?

DANTLY: Yeah, one in the back. It was aching so I sorta yanked on it. It came right out. See?

(DANTLY shows BURRIS his tooth.)

BURRIS: Wow. Did it hurt?

DANTLY: Not really. It made me sad more than anything.

BURRIS: So your tooth fell out and then you shaved your ass.

DANTLY: Change is good, right?

BURRIS: Yeah, change is totally good.

DANTLY: I feel sorta new. Like a new man.

BURRIS: That's so excellent, Walt. *(He crosses to the mirror, fixes his hair.)*

BURRIS: I wonder if that chick from the head shop's gonna stop by.

DANTLY: She won't.

BURRIS: How do you know?

DANTLY: Chicks never just stop by.

BURRIS: She might, she really might. What was her name, anyway?

DANTLY: Cassandra.

BURRIS: That's right, Cassandra. Man, she was fucking hot. Great tits. Great gams. I hope she stops by.

DANTLY: Don't count on it.

BURRIS: You never know, man. Fucking small town like this. Nowhere to go. Nothing to do. Couple of sophisticated guys from New York come through. Guys with cool clothes and a stalwart way. Hey, those kinda chicks are always looking for a way out. Salvation or whatever.

DANTLY: She seemed nervous.

BURRIS: Of course she seemed nervous. She liked you, man.

DANTLY: Yeah?

BURRIS: Yeah.

DANTLY: I could stick by a girl like that. Nice skin. Good hair.

BURRIS: Fuck her skin and her hair. What about the hams and the gams? The hams, gams and shanks, huh? That's where the money's at.

DANTLY: I guess.

ACT ONE

BURRIS: You *guess*? You *know*, man. That right there is a hard fact. That's like *species* truth.

DANTLY: Um. What's stalwart?

BURRIS: Stalwart is rugged, man. Brawny. Like muscular or whatever. I wish I had a cigarette.

(The phone rings twice. They stare at the phone. BURRIS *answers it.)*

BURRIS: Hello? ...Hello? ...Is that you, Zankich? ...Zankich? *(He stares at the receiver and then hangs up.)*

DANTLY: The breathing again?

*(*BURRIS *nods.)*

DANTLY: Like someone's sleepin, right?

BURRIS: Sort of, yeah.

DANTLY: Where did Zankich say these shrooms were coming from, anyway?

BURRIS: I think Amsterdam. Why?

DANTLY: Why would we have to come all the way down to fucking Boone, North Carolina to move a pound and a half of mushrooms from Amsterdam?

BURRIS: It's a college town.

DANTLY: So?

BURRIS: Whattaya mean, so? This place is so hippied-out it's practically a Renaissance Festival. Would ye like a leg of lamb or whatever. You saw the people in that head shop. The beads. The facial hair. The fucking corduroy.

DANTLY: So what's your point?

BURRIS: My point is that this heavily undergraduate municipality is a prime market for shrooms and various other drugs of psychedelic proportions. Whoever divvies the stuff up before Zankich takes his pound-and-a-half probably lives around here. I'll bet it's a hub.

DANTLY: You think?

BURRIS: I totally think.

DANTLY: Burris, I'd just like to say somethin.

BURRIS: What.

DANTLY: Sometimes you use words for your own recreational boner.

BURRIS: Really.

DANTLY: Yeah. And when it's just you and me it's cool, but when you go out that door there it can get off-putting. Like the way you were talkin to that guy at the head shop. The professor. The guy with the beard.

BURRIS: How was I talking to that guy at the head shop?

DANTLY: Dan, you were like pulling these forty-dollar words out of the waistband of your underwear.

BURRIS: I was?

DANTLY: You used the word truculent.

BURRIS: So?

DANTLY: Nobody knows what that word means.

BURRIS: Sure they do.

DANTLY: It's like a word out of a book, man. A book or a fucking crossword puzzle.

BURRIS: People know words.

DANTLY: No they don't, Dan. They totally don't.

BURRIS: That dude was a professor, man.

DANTLY: *You* probably don't even know what it means.

BURRIS: I know what it means.

ACT ONE

DANTLY: What does it mean?

BURRIS: I totally know what it means.

DANTLY: Do you?

BURRIS: It means viscous.

DANTLY: *Viscous?*

BURRIS: Yeah, viscous. Like snotty. Like boogery translucence.

DANTLY: Boogery translucence?

BURRIS: Yeah.

DANTLY: Daniel, truculent does not mean boogery translucence.

BURRIS: Sure it does.

DANTLY: No it doesn't.

BURRIS: It does too.

DANTLY: It does not.

BURRIS: It so does.

DANTLY: It so doesn't.

BURRIS: Yes it does.

DANTLY: It does not, man! *(He removes a piece of paper from his pocket.)*

DANTLY: Truculent: It means fierce. Cruel. Savagely brutal. Brutally harsh. Vitriolic. Scathing. His truculent criticisms of her work. Aggressively hostile. Belligerent. Savage. Pitiless. Not vicious.

BURRIS: Viscous.

DANTLY: Not viscous.

BURRIS: Let me see that.

(DANTLY *hands* BURRIS *the piece of paper.* BURRIS *studies it.*)

BURRIS: You ripped this out of a dictionary.

DANTLY: So?

BURRIS: Where'd you get it?

DANTLY: From the motel office. I stopped in when I went looking for the snow shovel.

BURRIS: You went like scouring the countryside for a dictionary? Like all obsessed and shit?

DANTLY: I felt I needed to know.

BURRIS: The office had a fucking dictionary?

DANTLY: I'm only tellin you cause we're friends. I've wanted to talk to you about it for a while now.

(BURRIS *reads the piece of paper again, balls it up, throws it on the bed, crosses to the window, stares out.*)

DANTLY: Dan?

(No answer)

DANTLY: Daniel.

BURRIS: What.

DANTLY: You okay?

BURRIS: I'm fine.

DANTLY: You sure?

BURRIS: You totally like hunted down a dictionary.

DANTLY: Oh, man, I'm sorry, Dan. I didn't mean to hurt your feelings.

BURRIS: You want me to like pare down my language. One of the few things I'm good at.

DANTLY: You're good at other things.

ACT ONE

BURRIS: Like what?

DANTLY: You're good with chicks. You're way better with them than I am. And you're good at pool.

BURRIS: I guess.

DANTLY: I've seen you run the table. Like that night at that fucking hick bar in Dubuque, Iowa.

BURRIS: Gomer's.

DANTLY: Yeah, Gomer's. You totally ran the table. And that pretty girl with the floppy hat came back to our hotel with us.

BURRIS: Angie.

DANTLY: Yeah, Angie. Man, she was pretty. She had that hat.

BURRIS: She was only seventeen. She bled all over the carpet.

DANTLY: The point is, you ran the table and then you got the chick. Pool and chicks. Two things you're really good at.

BURRIS: What the fuck were we doing in Dubuque, Iowa anyway?

DANTLY: Zankich sent us to pick up that shitload of ecstasy.

BURRIS: That's right. We drove like eighteen fucking hours.

DANTLY: Yeah, you almost swerved off the road like seven times. I was so nervous I don't even remember Ohio.

BURRIS: Yeah, the Midwest gives me the creeps. All those fat people.

(Pause)

DANTLY: That girl used to call you, didn't she?

BURRIS: Who, that chick from Dubuque?

DANTLY: Yeah. Angie.

BURRIS: Yeah, she called for a while.

DANTLY: But you never called her back.

BURRIS: She was too young, man. Too fucking tight for me.

DANTLY: I liked her.

BURRIS: You did?

DANTLY: Yeah. I thought there was something special about her. Her eyes.

BURRIS: What about her eyes?

DANTLY: They were so brown. Like Cocoa Crispies. I like that.

BURRIS: Well, I still got her number if you wanna give her a call.

DANTLY: You do?

BURRIS: Sure. You wanna call her?

DANTLY: I'd call her.

(BURRIS *removes a little black book from the back pocket of his strewn jeans, flips to a page.*)

BURRIS: It's right here. Angie McGrath. Three-one-nine, six- four-six, seven-eight-two-one. You should call her, Walt.

DANTLY: You really think so?

BURRIS: Yeah, man. She'd probably be really into you. She kept saying how she liked big guys. You heard her say that, am I right?

DANTLY: Yeah.

BURRIS: And you're a helluva lot bigger than me.

DANTLY: Yeah, I remember you tellin her that.

BURRIS: Telling her what.

DANTLY: How big I am.

BURRIS: I was talkin about your dick, Walt.

DANTLY: You were talking about my dick?

BURRIS: Yeah, I was telling her how big and fat your cock is.

DANTLY: Oh.

BURRIS: So call her.

(BURRIS *hands* DANTLY *the book.* DANTLY *takes it, turns to the phone, about to dial.*)

DANTLY: Maybe not.

BURRIS: Come on, man. Whattaya got to lose?

DANTLY: Nah.

BURRIS: What the fuck is wrong with you? You never do anything! Fucking do something for once!

(DANTLY *utters some sort of sound that speaks to humiliation, failure, and apology.*)

BURRIS: Fuck it. I'll call her. (*He takes the book back, moves to the phone, dials, waits.*)

BURRIS: Hello, is Angie there? Oh, this is Walter Dantly, a friend from out of town... Sure... Hello, Angie? This is um Walt Dantly. I met you last year when I was holidaying in Dubuque with my friend Dan Burris. Do you remember me? ...Dan Burris. I'm Walt Dantly. We met you at Gomer's. We played pool. You hung out with us at the Motel Six... Yeah, the big guy, that's me... *Hi*... Yeah, I'm a friend of Dan's...Dan Burris...Dan the-guy-with-the-big-vocabulary Dan... Oh, he's good.

Yeah, I just saw him yesterday. He was on his way
to Mexico. He's going um sword fishing in Cancun.
Sword fishing in the Gulf, yep... We met you at
Gomer's. You had that floppy hat on. Yeah, I'm Walt...
Dantly. I was the sort of big guy with the funny head...
You remember me, right? ...Cool... I'm fine, just fine.
How are you? ...Oh sure, sure. *(To* DANTLY*)* She's
closing her door. *(To the phone)* Hey... What am I
wearing? Um, well, at the moment it appears that
I'm wearing some faded J C Penny plain pockets,
an old pair of wool socks, and a long-sleeved T-shirt
that features a picture of a rather feisty-looking squirrel
with human testicles.

(DANTLY *inspects himself, realizes he is wearing the very T-shirt, pants and socks.)*

BURRIS: Why? What are *you* wearing, Angie? ...Uh-huh... Uh-huh... Uh- huh... That sounds very nice.

(BURRIS *crosses to* DANTLY *with the phone, quickly hands it to him.)*

DANTLY: Uh-huh... Uh-huh... Um, I don't know, kissing,
I guess... No... No... No... I don't know, Angie... Yeah,
I like motorcycles... Um, butter's cool... Pickles...
Do I like your what? ...Oh, sure. Sure, I like that.
That's cool... Uh-huh... Oh, right on... Hey, Angie,
do you remember how the three of us were at the drive-
through window of that Hardee's and you looked over
and you had that sparkle stuff on your cheeks and
I sorta kept giving you the thumbs-up sign? ...The
thumbs-up sign. Like you know... You don't? ...Well,
you were in the front seat with Burris and I was in the
back and you kept lookin over your shoulder and I
would give you a thumbs-up... Yeah, Burris... Dan...
He's good. He's down in Mexico... Yeah, sure, I'll tell
him to call you when he gets back.

But anyway, the point is that I was sending you a um
thumbs-up cause, well, cause I like really liked you...

Yeah, thumbs-up, that's my thing. See, you had those sparkles on your cheeks and when I like someone... Oh, really? ...Is he mad? ...Maybe I could call you later... Okay... I'll call you later... No, I'm not eatin anything... Oh, well my voice jumps around a little, depending on like my um saliva level... Sure, sure... Okay. *(He hangs up.)* I think she wanted to have phone sex.

BURRIS: Of course she wanted to have phone sex! What happened?! She was totally horny for your cock, man!

DANTLY: She asked me if I liked her jazzhole.

BURRIS: She did?!

DANTLY: Yeah.

BURRIS: That's so cool, Dantly!

DANTLY: It is?

BURRIS: Yeah!

DANTLY: What's a jazzhole?

BURRIS: Her anus, man!

DANTLY: Oh.

BURRIS: That's so fucking kinky!

DANTLY: I thought a jazzhole was a Jacuzzi.

BURRIS: *Jazzhole.* I *love* that!

DANTLY: It was your voice she liked, anyway. She got all suspicious when I took over.

BURRIS: But you played it off so well with that bit about your saliva level.

DANTLY: You think so?

BURRIS: I totally think so. So what happened?

DANTLY: She said her dad was knockin on her door.

BURRIS: Well that sucks... Are you gonna call her back?

DANTLY: I don't know.

BURRIS: Call her back, man!

DANTLY: Dan, I think I'd feel a little weird jerking off in fronta you.

BURRIS: I'd go in the bathroom.

DANTLY: Still, it'd be a little weird. I mean, I'd be out here with a full-fledged boner.

BURRIS: Walt, it's not like I haven't seen your dick before.

DANTLY: But what if you accidentally came out when I started like spurting my pearly jism all over your face...I mean the place. Like if you needed your Right Guard or whatever.

BURRIS: I wouldn't need my Right Guard. I've already Right Guarded my balls today. And moreover, I'd wait. I'd even give you the appropriate amount of time to clean up.

DANTLY: It would be way too complicated. And besides, it's still a little tender. From the ice scraper.

BURRIS: Oh. Right on.

DANTLY: And I'd like to see if Cassandra's gonna come by. Cause she might, right?

BURRIS: She totally might. You want me to go get her? I could go get her.

DANTLY: You would?

BURRIS: Yeah.

DANTLY: You'd go all the way down to the head shop?

BURRIS: It's only like six blocks. I'll go right now.

DANTLY: Really? You'd do that?

BURRIS: Of course, man.

ACT ONE

DANTLY: Okay.

BURRIS: Excellent. But Walt, if I were you I'd stay away from that thumbs-up business. I don't think chicks dig that kinda thing. I'll just get my stuff on.

DANTLY: Be cool about it this time, okay?

BURRIS: Sure. *(He crosses to the corner, unseen, returns wearing a pair of black bikini briefs. He steps into his jeans, layers on a vest, a pair of boots.)*

DANTLY: Hey, Burris?

BURRIS: Huh.

DANTLY: Do you remember what that guy at the head shop was talkin about?

BURRIS: Who?

DANTLY: The guy with the beard. The professor. When you were checking out that iron bong he said somethin to you about the snow and you told him to have a truculent day and he looked at you funny.

BURRIS: Oh yeah, the guy with the students. All those little college chicks in big sweatshirts. What was he talking about?

DANTLY: The like Divine Order of Things.

BURRIS: Oh yeah, The Divine Order of Things.

DANTLY: God, angels, humans, animals, plants, rocks. That's what he said, right?

BURRIS: I'm not sure, Dantly. There might have been a fish or like a bird involved, too. Or U F Os. And you can't forget the little creatures. Like insects or whatever.

DANTLY: What about snow?

BURRIS: What about it?

DANTLY: You think it falls in there somewhere?

BURRIS: Um. I doubt it. Snow is like water.

DANTLY: But they include rocks.

BURRIS: But rocks are rocks, man. Not water.

DANTLY: But like icebergs are sorta rocky. Or bread. What about bread?

BURRIS: You're like totally tripping out, man.

DANTLY: Well, I was just thinking about how I don't know where I fit in. Like I know that I'm biographically human or whatever, but I think I feel more like a plant.

BURRIS: Biologically.

DANTLY: Huh?

BURRIS: Biologically. You said biographically.

DANTLY: I did?

BURRIS: Yeah, man... So you feel like a plant. You feel plant-like.

DANTLY: I do. Like a fern. Or one of those things in the desert.

BURRIS: A cactus?

DANTLY: Yeah, one of those. How they just like sit there.

BURRIS: Um, I wouldn't burn too many calories over it, Walt. I mean, you're a red-blooded mammal, right?

DANTLY: I guess.

BURRIS: You eat, you sleep, you void your bowels, am I wrong? Plants are like into light and soil and water. Photosynthesis or whatever. You're a meat-eater.

DANTLY: Yeah, but I'm not like *thought* about. For instance, if I'm lookin at somethin on a shelf. Like a rock or stick or a plate of sausage or whatever, I forget about it when I leave the room. The stuff on the shelf doesn't stay with me. I'm like that.

ACT ONE

BURRIS: But what does that mean, Walt?

DANTLY: It means that I don't like take up space in anybody's head.

BURRIS: Yes you do.

DANTLY: No I don't.

BURRIS: Sure you do, man.

DANTLY: Whose head? Who thinks about me, Dan?

BURRIS: *I* think about you. Fucking *Zankich* thinks about you!

DANTLY: Yeah, maybe when we're in the car together. Or like if you have to borrow my toothpaste and we run into each other in the bathroom. But when I'm not around I might as well be a plant, and that's my point.

BURRIS: Look, Walt. Meat eater to meat eater. We totally think about you. We're mammals. Our mothers breastfeed us from their great maternal teats. Do you get what I'm saying?

DANTLY: Sure.

BURRIS: Well, I really don't know what more to say about all this so I'm gonna go, okay? ...Okay, Walt?

DANTLY: Okay.

BURRIS: So take it easy. *(He puts on a huge silver snow parka, pulls a black ski mask over his head, fully dressed now.)*

BURRIS: So I'm gonna go secure Cassandra.

DANTLY: Tell her I say hey.

BURRIS: I will. I'll tell her that. You might wanna pick this place up a bit. Maybe stack those pizza boxes.

DANTLY: Okay.

BURRIS: Wish me luck.

DANTLY: Good luck, Burris.

BURRIS: Thanks, Dantly.

(Pause)

DANTLY: Hey, Dan.

BURRIS: Yeah?

DANTLY: I feel like somethin bad's gonna go down.

BURRIS: Oh. Why?

DANTLY: Cause this thing keeps happening.

BURRIS: What thing.

DANTLY: Every time I close my eyes I see this grizzly bear.

BURRIS: You do?

DANTLY: Yeah, one of those big ones with the claws. I close my eyes and there it is.

BURRIS: You need to get some sleep, man. When was the last time you slept?

DANTLY: I feel like we should load the gun.

BURRIS: Nothing's gonna go down, Dantly.

DANTLY: Where's the money?

(BURRIS *moves to the bed, reaches under it, removes a brown paper bag full of money, shows* DANTLY.)

DANTLY: It's a lot of money.

BURRIS: Nobody knows about it.

DANTLY: You sure?

BURRIS: We're in bumfuck Boone, man. *(He puts the money back.)*

DANTLY: I don't know if I can trust you lately.

BURRIS: What? Why?

ACT ONE

DANTLY: I don't know. I think it's cause of this dream I had when we were down in Sarasota.

BURRIS: What dream?

DANTLY: Me and you were astronauts. We had these big silver suits on. We were in space. We had lost our ship and we were floating through this like sphere of alien launching pads. There was a very gloomy tone to the dream. I got a hole in the back of my suit and you went behind me to patch it with some like gravity caulking or whatever, but instead of fixing it you tried to stick your finger up my butt.

BURRIS: Really.

DANTLY: Uh-huh.

BURRIS: Wow.

DANTLY: I know, right?

BURRIS: ...What the fuck is gravity caulking?

DANTLY: Like that stuff you use to seal windows.

(BURRIS *lifts the ski mask.*)

BURRIS: Um, Walt?

DANTLY: Yeah?

BURRIS: I promise you with every cell of honor in my heroic body that I do not want to stick my finger up your butt. Just take it easy. Okay?

DANTLY: Okay.

(BURRIS *pulls the ski mask back down over his face, opens the door. The snow is horizontal. He exits, closing the door behind him.*)

(DANTLY *remains in the bed, watching T V. The phone rings. He answers it.*)

DANTLY: Hello? ...Hello?

(He stares at the phone, then hangs up. He watches the T V, then grabs the remote and turns it off. He puts the remote down his pants. He waits. After a moment, he removes the remote, gets out of the bed, collects a few pizza boxes, stacks them in the corner, puts an ab roller back in BURRIS' *bag. From the bag he removes a large aerosol spray container of Right Guard. He moves in front of the mirror, stares at himself. He then drops his pants and underwear. There is a small piece of blood-spotted tissue paper stuck to one of his butt cheeks.)*

(He lifts his scrotum tenderly, and sprays an enormous amount of Right Guard under his balls. He then releases his scrotum and stands there.)

(Suddenly the bathroom door opens and a man appears. He is incredibly tall, at least six-six, and very thin. He is wearing large boots, threadbare briefs, a stained T-shirt, and a headband with a feather. He is holding a potted cactus. They stare at each other. The man sets the plant next to the T V and then produces a single, blue-tip camping match and strikes it against the wall, lighting it. He holds it out in front of him, until the flame drops down to his fingers. After the match burns out, he removes a small cellphone from one of his pockets, dials a number. The motel room phone rings. DANTLY *stares at it, then at the man. After a few rings, he crosses to the phone, answers it.)*

DANTLY: Hello?

MAN: Would ye like a leg of lamb?

(The man closes his cellphone, then crosses to the front door, opens it, and walks out into the snow. DANTLY *sets the phone down, crosses to the entrance and stares out, then closes the door and pulls his pants up. He stares out the window. The phone rings again. He crosses to the phone, sits on the bed, watches it, then answers it.)*

DANTLY: Hello? ...Hello? ...Who are you?

(DANTLY *stares at the phone in his hand, hangs it up. He crosses to* BURRIS' *bag, reaches into it and removes a nine-millimeter, loads it, crosses back to the bed, stares at it in his hand, then puts it down his pants. Alarmed, he removed the nine-millimeter from his pants. He ejects the clip, puts it in his pocket, then places the nine millimeter back down his pants. He sits there, removes his tooth from his other pocket, stares at it in his hand.)*

END OF ACT ONE

ACT TWO

(Three hours later. DANTLY is sprawled on the bed, dead asleep. The blinds have been pulled. The cactus has been set on the bedside stand. A young woman, CASSANDRA, is seated in a chair watching him, a suitcase set at her feet. She is pretty, nervous, lost somehow. She wears a snow parka, beads in her hair, an old T-shirt, corduroys, Birkenstock sandals without socks, toe rings, an ankle bracelet. She fidgets, reaches into her coat pocket, removes an empty pack of American Spirits blues. It appears that she has been there a while. The phone rings. DANTLY stirs, wakes, stares at the phone. The phone stops ringing. He notices her. There is an awkward silence.)

CASSANDRA: Hey.

DANTLY: Hey. *(He removes the remote from down his pants, sets it on the bedside stand. He removes his room key from down his pants, sets it on the bedside stand.)*

CASSANDRA: Got a cigarette?

DANTLY: I don't smoke. *(He reaches into his pants, removes the nine millimeter, opens the drawer to the bedside stand, places it inside, closes the drawer.)*

CASSANDRA: Do you always keep things down your pants?

DANTLY: It's just a phase.

CASSANDRA: Phases are good.

(Pause)

DANTLY: Cassandra, right?

CASSANDRA: Yep.

DANTLY: Hey.

CASSANDRA: Hey.

DANTLY: You work at the head shop.

CASSANDRA: I do. You gave me your number, remember?

DANTLY: Yeah. Did you try calling here earlier?

CASSANDRA: No. But I thought about it. I brought you something. Here. *(From her pocket she removes a small stone figure, hands it to him.)*

DANTLY: What is it?

CASSANDRA: It's a bear bong. We sell them at the shop. It's sort of a local thing. We get a lot of brown bear that come down from the mountains. Around here they're considered sacred creatures.

DANTLY: Thanks. It looks hungry.

CASSANDRA: They're actually pretty friendly as long as you don't piss them off.

DANTLY: How long have you been—

CASSANDRA: Not long.

DANTLY: How'd you—

CASSANDRA: Door was open.

DANTLY: Oh.

CASSANDRA: You were sleeping.

(Suddenly DANTLY stands in the middle of the bed, looks down his pants, then sits, confused.)

CASSANDRA: Are you okay?

DANTLY: I was remembering this dream I just had.

ACT TWO

CASSANDRA: What was it about?

DANTLY: Well, I was sleeping right here in this bed. In my dream.

CASSANDRA: So you were dreaming that you were sleeping.

DANTLY: Yeah. I was sleeping and then I woke up.

CASSANDRA: You *dreamed* that you woke up.

DANTLY: Uh-huh. I woke up and I stood on the bed and took my pants down to check my um penis.

CASSANDRA: Oh.

DANTLY: Because I had injured it earlier that day.

CASSANDRA: You injured it earlier that day in the dream or earlier that day in real life.

DANTLY: In real life.

CASSANDRA: That must be the ice scraper thing, right?

DANTLY: Um. Uh-huh.

CASSANDRA: Yeah, Dan told me about that. Keep going.

DANTLY: So in my dream I like stood up. In the middle of this bed. And I took my pants down. But my penis had like um turned into a Nerf ball.

CASSANDRA: Weird.

DANTLY: I know, right?

CASSANDRA: Like a Nerf football?

DANTLY: No. Like one of those little round ones.

CASSANDRA: Cute. So what happened?

DANTLY: Well, then another one of me opened the door.

CASSANDRA: So you doubled.

DANTLY: Yeah, I doubled. And the me in the door had this little strip of Velcro taped to his forehead. And I walked up to him.

CASSANDRA: You walked up to the You in the doorway.

DANTLY: Yeah, I walked up to the Me in the doorway and I removed my Nerf ball penis and I like attached it to his forehead.

CASSANDRA: You stuck your penis to your own forehead.

DANTLY: To the forehead of the Me in the doorway, yeah.

CASSANDRA: There are so many levels to that.

DANTLY: The weird thing is that when I removed the Nerf ball there wasn't anything there. There wasn't a strip of Velcro or a piece of cardboard or anything. There was just this like void.

CASSANDRA: Interesting.

DANTLY: The other weird thing is that the Me in the doorway had better hair... What do you think it means?

CASSANDRA: I don't know. What do you think it means?

DANTLY: I'm not sure. But I'm pretty certain it has something to do with my penis. Excuse me.

(DANTLY *creeps to the front door, opens it very quickly.* CASSANDRA *stands suddenly, turns away. The snow is horizontal. He closes the door, then crosses back to the bed, stands, looks down his pants.*)

CASSANDRA: Is it still there?

DANTLY: Uh-huh.

CASSANDRA: Well that's a good sign.

(DANTLY *lays back down on the bed.* CASSANDRA *sits.*)

ACT TWO   41

DANTLY: I'm Walt.

CASSANDRA: I know.

DANTLY: You do?

CASSANDRA: Yeah, Dan told me.

DANTLY: Oh.

CASSANDRA: Yep. He told me all about you.

DANTLY: He did?

CASSANDRA: Uh-huh.

DANTLY: Wow. What'd he tell you?

CASSANDRA: Just stuff. You sound like a very interesting person. I've never met an Olympic lugist before.

DANTLY: Huh.

CASSANDRA: Aerodynamics are sexy.

DANTLY: They are?

CASSANDRA: There's nothing like the feeling of fast air against your skin. Woosh, you know?

DANTLY: Woosh?

CASSANDRA: Yeah, you are the wind beneath my wings.

DANTLY: I am?

CASSANDRA: That's from that movie *Beaches*. You like movies?

DANTLY: Sometimes.

CASSANDRA: What's your favorite movie?

DANTLY: I don't know.

CASSANDRA: Come on. Everyone has a favorite movie.

DANTLY: I like that movie called The Champ. About the boxer. The little kid cries a lot. And I like those Christmas specials. The ones with the clay.

CASSANDRA: Oh, I love those.

DANTLY: There's that one with the toy maker who wants to grow up to be a dentist.

CASSANDRA: Rudolph the Red-Nosed Reindeer!

DANTLY: Yeah, Rudolph the Red-Nosed Reindeer! Did you ever see it?

CASSANDRA: It's one of my all-time favorites.

DANTLY: Really?

CASSANDRA: Yeah!

DANTLY: Wow. Do you remember the part when all the yearlings are getting ready for takeoff practice and Rudolf meets that doe?

CASSANDRA: Clarice.

DANTLY: Yeah, Clarice. She has that little bow. It's red with white polka dots.

CASSANDRA: A doe bow.

DANTLY: A doe bow, right! And Rudolph's about to ask her if he can walk her home after takeoff practice—

CASSANDRA: And Clarice tells him he's cute.

DANTLY: Yeah, Clarice tells him he's cute! And then Rudolph gets so excited he starts to spontaneously combust *I mean fly*. And he starts going, I'm cute! I'm cute! But then when he lands his fake nose pops off and he gets all sad and says he wasn't very lucky today and then she sings this song called There's Always Tomorrow do you remember that?

CASSANDRA: That's my favorite part.

ACT TWO

DANTLY: It is?!

CASSANDRA: Yeah. It's such a beautiful moment.

DANTLY: I know, right?! There's those bunnies and the raccoons! And the little red birds that keep swooping down! I know the song!

CASSANDRA: You do?

DANTLY: Yeah! I've memorized it! Should I like sing it?

CASSANDRA: Um. Sure.

DANTLY: Really?! Cause it's like one of the greatest songs ever written, Cassandra.

CASSANDRA: You should sing it.

DANTLY: You think?

CASSANDRA: Yeah, I'd really like that.

DANTLY: Okay. *(He clears his throat and sings with great feeling.)* There's always tomorrow
For dreams to come true
Believe in your dreams come what may
There's always tomorrow
With so much to do
And so little time in a day

(A silence)

CASSANDRA: That was really great, Walt.

DANTLY: Really?

CASSANDRA: Yeah, you have an amazing voice. It's so soulful.

DANTLY: Wow... You think it's soulful?

CASSANDRA: Absolutely.

DANTLY: Do you wanna sing it with me? Cause there's a whole other part about this rainbow.

CASSANDRA: Maybe later.

DANTLY: Okay.

CASSANDRA: We'll save it.

DANTLY: Oh. Right on.

(Pause)

CASSANDRA: You're cute.

(Awkward pause)

DANTLY: Yeah the kid who wants to be the dentist. His name is Herby. He tries really hard. I like his style.

CASSANDRA: Style points.

DANTLY: Huh?

CASSANDRA: I do that sometimes. Take the last word someone says and free-associate. It keeps the conversation going. *(Pause)* When I came in you were sleeping like someone who gets pulled out of a car crash.

DANTLY: I was?

CASSANDRA: Yeah, for a minute I thought you were dead.

DANTLY: I haven't been sleeping much lately. Every time I close my eyes—

CASSANDRA: You see a grizzly bear, I know.

DANTLY: How do you know?

CASSANDRA: I just do.

DANTLY: Did Dan tell you that, too?

CASSANDRA: He told me it was a moose. But I knew it was a grizzly bear. You know they say if a man sits still enough in the presence of a bear that the bear will talk to him?

DANTLY: Really?

ACT TWO

CASSANDRA: Yep.

DANTLY: Like in English?

CASSANDRA: In the voice of the man. Pretty cool, huh? It's an old Indian belief.

DANTLY: Huh... Where is Burris, anyway? *(He is drawn to the cactus.)*

CASSANDRA: He went looking for a shovel. To dig out your car.

DANTLY: Oh. It's still snowing?

CASSANDRA: Yeah. It's not gonna stop for a while.

DANTLY: How do you know?

CASSANDRA: I just do.

(Pause)

CASSANDRA: So Dan told me that you're thinking about changing your name.

DANTLY: He did?

CASSANDRA: Yep. What do you want to change it to?

DANTLY: I don't know. Maybe Dave.

CASSANDRA: I like Walt better.

DANTLY: You do?

CASSANDRA: Yeah. Sounds like a chef's name.

DANTLY: It does?

CASSANDRA: Yeah, it's cheffy. I like chefs.

DANTLY: Huh.

(Pause)

CASSANDRA: You have a thing for plants.

DANTLY: Excuse me?

CASSANDRA: What.

DANTLY: I don't have anything down my pants.

CASSANDRA: I said you have a thing for *plants*.

DANTLY: Oh. Sorry. I thought... Sorry.

CASSANDRA: It's just that you keep staring at that plant. And I happen to know for a fact that these rooms don't come with vegetation.

DANTLY: How do you know that?

CASSANDRA: Cause I lived here for a few months. They don't give you plants and they don't give you those little bars of soap.

DANTLY: When did you live here?

CASSANDRA: After I quit school. It was a weird time, you know?

DANTLY: Where do you live now?

CASSANDRA: I rent an apartment over by the head shop. Me and this other girl. Well she's dead now so it's just me now.

DANTLY: Oh.

CASSANDRA: When I lived here I really wanted this room. This is the Daniel Boone Room, did you know that?

DANTLY: Nu-uh.

CASSANDRA: Well, I wanted this room. It has good vibrations. A sense of destiny. But my husband was living in the Davy Crockett Room. The Davy Crockett Room has broadband.

DANTLY: So you have a husband?

CASSANDRA: Well, we're still officially married but I left him because he started lighting things on fire.

DANTLY: Oh. Does he like work here?

CASSANDRA: No. He just lives here. He's really tall. Skinny. He's sort of magical.

DANTLY: I think I met him.

CASSANDRA: If he finds out I'm here he'll probably try and kill me, so you'll have to be my bodyguard.

DANTLY: Okay.

CASSANDRA: Yeah, there's a real sense of destiny in this room. Do you believe in destiny?

DANTLY: That's like fate, right?

CASSANDRA: Yeah.

DANTLY: I used to think about that stuff.

CASSANDRA: But you don't anymore?

DANTLY: Not really. I mean, sometimes I'll see myself in certain ways. Like skating on a frozen lake. Or being at the circus. Elephants. The human cannonball. Big blobs of cotton candy. But that's as far as I go with Destiny.

CASSANDRA: When I think of destiny I think of death.

DANTLY: What, like *death* death?

CASSANDRA: Yeah, like how we die. Where we'll be. What position we'll end up in. The expression on our face.

DANTLY: I used to watch the Cubs on T V. W G N channel nine. They were always the worst team in baseball. But there was this one guy. Dave Kingman. He would hit these home runs so far the ball would like turn into a bird. They called him King Kong.
   I used to keep his baseball card in my back pocket. I would like take it out and memorize stuff. Like the stats or whatever. When he got traded it was like he died. I used to imagine his face. The way it looked on his baseball card. He had a mustache. Dave Kingman.

CASSANDRA: Is he dead?

DANTLY: I don't know. It seems that way.

CASSANDRA: Do you still have the card?

DANTLY: I flung it off a bridge.

(Pause)

CASSANDRA: I like plants. Nature, you know?

DANTLY: Sure.

CASSANDRA: Are you a nature buff?

DANTLY: What?

CASSANDRA: A nature buff. Are you a nature buff?

DANTLY: Oh, I thought you said something else.

CASSANDRA: What did you think I said?

DANTLY: I thought you asked if I had natural buns.

CASSANDRA: Do you?

DANTLY: What.

CASSANDRA: Have natural buns.

DANTLY: Um. Pretty much.

CASSANDRA: I'll bet.

(Pause)

CASSANDRA: So Dan told me that you gave up your career in the luge so that you can work with kids.

DANTLY: He did?

CASSANDRA: Yeah, I really admire that.

DANTLY: Burris told you I work with kids?

CASSANDRA: He said you work with children who survive car crashes. That's what you do, right?

DANTLY: Well, it's not just kids. I work with um professional stock car racers, too.

CASSANDRA: Sounds exciting.

DANTLY: Hey, can I ask you a question?

CASSANDRA: You just did but ask me another one.

DANTLY: Okay. Um. Does it smell like farts in here to you?

CASSANDRA: No. It smells like Right Guard, actually. Right Guard and pizza.

DANTLY: Huh. What time is it, anyway?

CASSANDRA: I don't know. Late. We closed the bar.

DANTLY: You and Burris?

CASSANDRA: Yeah, Dan. He's funny and he eats a lot of beef jerky. I like mischievous guys.

DANTLY: You think he's mischievous?

CASSANDRA: Yeah. He's skinny, too. He showed me his stomach muscles.

DANTLY: He did?

CASSANDRA: He kept trying to get me to strum his six-pack.

DANTLY: Wow.

CASSANDRA: Yeah, Dan talks a lot. I like talkers. But you're quiet. I like quiet, too.

(Pause)

CASSANDRA: Dan told me about that thing you do.

DANTLY: What thing?

CASSANDRA: The thumbs-up thing. That's so cute.

(Awkward pause)

DANTLY: So, are you like a student?

CASSANDRA: Used to be. I stopped going to class a few semesters ago. Been working at the shop ever since.

DANTLY: Where you from?

CASSANDRA: Where do you think I'm from?

DANTLY: I don't know.

CASSANDRA: Take a guess.

DANTLY: Canada.

CASSANDRA: Guess again.

DANTLY: New Jersey.

CASSANDRA: Nope.

DANTLY: The North Pole.

CASSANDRA: Idaho.

DANTLY: That's a state, right?

CASSANDRA: Yeah, a state of depression. Where are you from?

DANTLY: Um, like a house.

CASSANDRA: Where was the house?

DANTLY: I don't know. Somewhere in the middle of things. It's weird. Since we've been on this trip I've been forgetting stuff. Like before I was thinkin about my tooth.

CASSANDRA: What about your tooth?

DANTLY: Well, it fell out earlier. It was aching so I sorta yanked on it. It came right out. I thought it would be some weird color. Like black or green or whatever. But it wasn't. It was white. I was thinkin how it was good that I didn't lose it in the snow. And I had this other thought about how our teeth are like...

ACT TWO

CASSANDRA: Like what?

DANTLY: ...See what I mean? I can't remember anything. I live in New York, now.

CASSANDRA: New York City?

DANTLY: Uh-huh.

CASSANDRA: I've always wanted to go to New York. Smoke a blunt. Ride in a taxi.

(Pause)

CASSANDRA: You don't move around much, do you?

DANTLY: You mean like around the country?

CASSANDRA: No I mean like around the room.

DANTLY: Not really.

CASSANDRA: It's just an observation. I observe things. That must be good for the luge. Not moving. *(She sits next to* DANTLY *on the bed.)* Do you get stiff?

DANTLY: Stiff?

CASSANDRA: Yeah, like your joints.

DANTLY: Not really.

CASSANDRA: I used to do Yoga at school, but I was too sensitive. Other people's energy, you know? It was intense. But I like the positions. I can get into some pretty interesting positions.

(Awkward pause)

CASSANDRA: I like your head.

DANTLY: You do?

CASSANDRA: Yeah, I like the shape of it. It's big.

DANTLY: Thanks.

CASSANDRA: You probably have a huge brain.

DANTLY: You think?

CASSANDRA: Yeah. Dogs have little brains. The size of a walnut. Dogs and squirrels...I'm telepathic. That's why I dropped out of school. Cause I knew too much. Think of a word.

DANTLY: Why.

CASSANDRA: Think of a word. I'll guess it.

(DANTLY *thinks.*)

CASSANDRA: Ready?

DANTLY: Uh-huh.

CASSANDRA: Don't cloud your thoughts with anything else, okay?

DANTLY: Okay.

(CASSANDRA *stares at* DANTLY.)

CASSANDRA: Truculent.

(DANTLY *stares at* CASSANDRA *in disbelief.*)

CASSANDRA: It's either truculent or succulent. I got it, right?

DANTLY: How'd you do that?

CASSANDRA: I can do state capitals and the last names of American presidents, too.

DANTLY: What about playing cards, can you do playing cards?

CASSANDRA: Only Jacks and Kings, nothing else. But I can do weather. And I know when somebody's gonna die.

DANTLY: How?

CASSANDRA: My breasts start leaking.

DANTLY: Wow.

ACT TWO

CASSANDRA: A few days ago my roommate killed herself with kitchen cleanser. While I was walking up the stairs my breasts were leaking so bad my whole stomach was damp. I knew she was dead before I even opened the door. People die every day, you know?

DANTLY: When you came in you thought *I* might be dead, but you knew I wasn't cause you weren't um leaking?

CASSANDRA: Uh-huh.

DANTLY: So you have these like totally milky boobs?

CASSANDRA: Yeah, I recently had a baby. A little boy.

DANTLY: Oh. Wow.

CASSANDRA: It came out dead but my body still does stuff. I was gonna name him Cecil. I donated him to the hospital so they could study things. They gave me fifty bucks.... I'd like to think that when babies come out dead they get born back into the world. Like their souls jump into other people. Do you believe in reincarnation?

DANTLY: I've never really thought about it.

CASSANDRA: Well, some people think that when we die our souls pass into new containers. Like a tree or a rock. Or animals. Even other humans.

DANTLY: That's sorta what that guy at the head shop was talking about. The Divine order of things.

CASSANDRA: That's right. The Divine Order of things.

DANTLY: I've been thinkin about that. God, angels, humans, animals, plants, rocks.

CASSANDRA: What about it?

DANTLY: Well, like about what it is that makes us different. I think I know.

CASSANDRA: What is it?

DANTLY: Well, take animals, for instance. They eat. They sleep. They seek shelter. And so do we. We meaning humans. The difference is that we have ideas. Like poems. Or holidays. Take a cat or a llama or a fucking wolf. They don't have that. They don't have ideas. They don't understand math or like words. They don't declare war. They don't write stuff down. I mean, I can see somethin in my head. Like a kite or a charbroiled steak. And then I can draw it with a crayon on a paper plate.

CASSANDRA: A *kite*-steak. Sounds interesting.

DANTLY: Yeah, I used to go to the zoo and watch the animals. It's complicated.

(Pause)

CASSANDRA: Professor Bailey's big into reincarnation. Animals mostly. But I think there's more to it. Clouds. Wind. Water.

DANTLY: What about snow?

CASSANDRA: Snow is water.

DANTLY: Oh, right... The problem with me is that I don't have any ideas. But I used to. I used to have some. And I hardly even eat anymore. That pizza was the first thing I'd eaten in like three days. And right afterwards my tooth fell out. What if I have cancer?

CASSANDRA: Maybe you're just sad.

DANTLY: Maybe.

CASSANDRA: What are you sad about?

DANTLY: I guess I have this fear—

CASSANDRA: That you don't take up space in anybody's head?

DANTLY: Yeah. Like I'm not *thought* about or whatever. How did you *know*—

ACT TWO 55

CASSANDRA: You're taking up space in my head.

DANTLY: I am?

CASSANDRA: Of course. You are right now. So don't be sad... Would you like to come back?

DANTLY: Come back from where?

CASSANDRA: The dead.

DANTLY: Um. Sure.

CASSANDRA: What would you want to be? The first thing that comes to your head.

DANTLY: A go-cart.

CASSANDRA: You were so uninhibited when you said that. You thought go-cart and you just said it. That's really sweet.

DANTLY: What would you come back as?

CASSANDRA: A chocolate waterfall! Like the one in Willy Wonka. Either a chocolate waterfall or a goose.

(Pause)

DANTLY: I never had any kids. I wonder what it would be like.

CASSANDRA: Cecil was the best thing that ever happened to me. I know he's out there somewhere.

DANTLY: I held a baby once. It was so small. It sounded like two pieces of Styrofoam rubbing together.

CASSANDRA: Whose baby was it?

DANTLY: I can't remember. I used to know. It was beautiful, though. Smallest hands I've ever seen in my life. Holding it made me feel huge. Like I could do anything.... Hey, can we do that word thing again?

CASSANDRA: Okay, but don't cloud your thoughts.

DANTLY: I won't.

CASSANDRA: And give me your hand this time.

(DANTLY *offers his hand.* CASSANDRA *takes it.*)

CASSANDRA: Got one?

DANTLY: Uh-huh.

(CASSANDRA *stares at* DANTLY *intently.*)

CASSANDRA: Leg of lamb.

DANTLY: You're amazing.

CASSANDRA: Sometimes I know too much. It gets me in trouble. That's why I smoke: it gives me something to do. *(Still holding his hand)* You know, Walt, we all have certain powers. It's just that some of us know how to tap into them. You have powers.

DANTLY: I do?

CASSANDRA: It starts with the will. Think of something for thirty seconds.

DANTLY: Like what?

CASSANDRA: Anything. Just think one singular thought for thirty seconds and I'll bet that later it will somehow manifest itself.

DANTLY: Like just say it over and over in my brain?

CASSANDRA: Picture it. I'll count to thirty. *(She releases his hand.)* Ready?

(DANTLY *grabs the bear bong, nods.*)

CASSANDRA: One, two, three, four...

(CASSANDRA *counts to thirty.* DANTLY *trembles with intensity, is nearly lifted out of the bed, reaches thirty, collapses, exhausted.*)

CASSANDRA: Congratulations. You just changed your life.

(A knock at the door)

CASSANDRA: Don't answer that.

DANTLY: Why not?

(Another knock)

DANTLY: Dan?

CASSANDRA: It's not Dan.

DANTLY: How do you know?

CASSANDRA: I just do.

DANTLY: Daniel?

(Another knock. Then the sound of footsteps fading in the snow)

DANTLY: Who was that?

CASSANDRA: My husband.

DANTLY: Whoa.

(CASSANDRA slowly crosses to the entrance, places her hand on the surface of the door, moves away, puts her coat on.)

CASSANDRA: Yeah, things change after you get pregnant. After Cecil came out dead I used to carry a balloon in my pocket. A little red one. I drew a face on it and everything. But one day my husband found it. He blew it up and popped it with a pin. By the way, what are you planning on doing with the gun in that drawer?

DANTLY: I don't know.

CASSANDRA: Have you ever shot anyone?

DANTLY: I shot a squirrel with a bee-bee gun once.

CASSANDRA: But would you shoot a person?

DANTLY: I guess if I had to I would. Why?

CASSANDRA: Just wondering.

(Pause)

DANTLY: Hey, do you know anything about a guy called The Burning Man?

CASSANDRA: Lemoyne.

DANTLY: Lemoyne?

CASSANDRA: Yeah, Lemoyne from Des Moines.

DANTLY: Is that your husband?

CASSANDRA: No. My husband's name is Buck. Buck's from Des Moines, too.

DANTLY: So Buck's the one who was in here earlier?

CASSANDRA: I don't know. Was he?

DANTLY: He's tall, really skinny, sort of intense-lookin?

CASSANDRA: Yeah, that's Buck.

DANTLY: He came out of the bathroom while I was Right Guarding my balls. He was holding that plant. He set it down over there and lit a match.

CASSANDRA: He was probably being polite.

DANTLY: Polite?

CASSANDRA: With the match. You said he was in the bathroom. He probably didn't want to stink up the place.

DANTLY: Oh.

CASSANDRA: Yeah, the toilet in the Davy Crockett Room doesn't work so he sneaks into other peoples' bathrooms. I used to do it all the time.

DANTLY: Before you said he likes to light things on fire.

CASSANDRA: Well, that's a whole different thing.

DANTLY: How is it different?

ACT TWO

CASSANDRA: Well, these guys from Charlotte hired him to burn down some buildings. So they could collect the insurance.

DANTLY: Where were the buildings?

CASSANDRA: I'm not supposed to talk about it.

DANTLY: So what does Lemoyne look like?

CASSANDRA: Like a human mosquito. He's got a lot of hair in his nose.

DANTLY: Why do they call him The Burning Man?

(The phone rings.)

CASSANDRA: Aren't you gonna answer it?

(DANTLY answers the phone.)

DANTLY: Hello?... Hey, Zankich... Good... Uh-huh... Yeah, it's snowing pretty bad.... Just sittin around, watchin pizza, eatin the T V... Yeah, we're good... Everything's okay... No, that guy hasn't been by yet. He must be runnin late cause of the storm... I hope tomorrow, if the snow lets up...Burris? Oh, he's out... Lookin for a snow shovel. Why, is somethin wrong? ...Uh-huh... Uh-huh... Oh... Well, I'll tell him to call you... Okay, Zankich. *(He hangs up.)*

CASSANDRA: Who's Zankich?

DANTLY: Just this guy we sorta work for. It's um part-time. In addition to the child car crash thing.

CASSANDRA: What do you do for him?

DANTLY: We like run errands.

CASSANDRA: What kind of errands?

DANTLY: Just errands.

(The phone rings again. DANTLY answers it.)

DANTLY: Hello?... Yeah, she's here.... Hang on a second *(To* CASSANDRA*)* It's for you.

(CASSANDRA *takes the phone, sits next to* DANTLY.*)*

CASSANDRA: Hello?... Hey... Just a friend... Maybe... How'd you know I was here?... No... No... No... I wouldn't do that if I were you. He's a very dangerous guy. He used to be an Olympic lugist!... Suit yourself...

(CASSANDRA *hands the phone to* DANTLY*. He hangs up.)*

DANTLY: Buck, huh?

CASSANDRA: Yep.

DANTLY: What'd he say?

CASSANDRA: He said he's coming over.

DANTLY: Oh.

CASSANDRA: With his machete.

DANTLY: He's got a machete?

CASSANDRA: He's down in the Davy Crockett Room sharpening the blade. He said he's gonna come over when he's finished.

DANTLY: Jesus.

CASSANDRA: It takes him about fifteen minutes to sharpen the blade. He probably still has to change into his Arabian Nights Fighting Slacks, too, so we'll have a little time. If you decide not to shoot him I would go for his left knee. He has a weak left knee. He hurt it bowling.

DANTLY: Okay.

CASSANDRA: Yeah, love is really weird. When I first met Buck I hated him. I couldn't even look at him. He disgusted me. But things happen. People like change shape. The bones. The hair. The walk. They

ACT TWO 61

say your body literally changes every seven years. How old are you, Walt?

DANTLY: Um. I sorta stopped counting at some point. I'm definitely older than I used to be.

CASSANDRA: Well, maybe you're in for a big change.

DANTLY: I wish Dan would come back.

CASSANDRA: Oh, he's not coming back.

DANTLY: He's not?

CASSANDRA: No. He said we were gonna meet him down in Mexico.

DANTLY: He did?

CASSANDRA: Yeah. After he dropped me off he went to go get a snow shovel so he could dig out the car. He said that you had these really kick-ass frequent flier miles for you and one other person but that you guys had agreed that he would drive down ahead of you so you could have a car for Cancun and Cozumel and how much of a shame it was that there was no one else to bring along and how it was such a terrible waste of frequent flier miles and that you were gonna stick around here for another day or two to settle up with the motel and heal from your ice scraper injury and that if things went well between us that you would maybe take me down there so we could join him.

He said that you were gonna take this two-week course in Mexican cuisine led by this famous chef from the Yucatan Peninsula and that the three of us would go sword fishing on his friend's yacht and that our bungalow was like fifty yards from the Gulf of Mexico. Pelicans! Fish tacos! White sand beaches! Avocado trees!

DANTLY: Huh.

CASSANDRA: Yeah, he said that *he* had a bag of cash and that *you* had a bag of cash and that the trip was

something you two had been planning for years.
He paid me fifty bucks to come talk to you.

DANTLY: He did?

CASSANDRA: Uh-huh. To like try you out.

DANTLY: To try me out?

CASSANDRA: To see if I'd be interested in the whole Mexico thing. I've always wanted to travel. Get out of Boone, you know? And I know a little Spanish. I used to be able to say the Our Father. *Padre nuestro que estas en el cielo* and all that.

DANTLY: Burris paid you fifty bucks to come talk to me?

CASSANDRA: Yeah, he said he was worried about you. That a third person would be really good to have along. And I tried you out and I think it would work.

DANTLY: You do?

CASSANDRA: Yeah. I think we'd be good travel partners... Don't you?

DANTLY: Sure.

CASSANDRA: You don't seem so sure. Is it because I talk too much? I normally don't talk so much, I'm just a little nervous since my roommate died. And that whole thing with Cecil.

DANTLY: It's just that I don't have a bag of cash.

CASSANDRA: You don't?

DANTLY: Nu-uh. And I don't have any frequent flier miles either.

CASSANDRA: Really?

DANTLY: I've only flown like twice in my life.

CASSANDRA: Oh. Well, that's funny.

(DANTLY *looks under the bed.*)

ACT TWO 63

CASSANDRA: What's wrong?

DANTLY: The money's gone.

CASSANDRA: Whose money?

DANTLY: Zankich's money.

CASSANDRA: I'm confused.

DANTLY: There was a brown paper bag under the bed. It was sposed to be used for somethin. Burris took it. It was all the money we had.

CASSANDRA: But he said you *both* had money.

DANTLY: He lied.

CASSANDRA: ...So there's no trip to Mexico?

DANTLY: No.

CASSANDRA: And there are no frequent flier miles.

DANTLY: There's nothing.

CASSANDRA: Oh. *(She nearly faints. She has to use the furniture to help herself.)*

DANTLY: I used to go to the zoo. The Bronx Zoo every Thursday. I'd go to the monkey house and watch the apes. They only put one ape in a cage. They have this thing they do. They like talk to each other with their eyes. Right through the cage. Like "Hey, how's it goin? You think we'll be gettin outta here anytime soon? Hang in there, buddy. Just hang in there". They have this like thing. A closeness. Or the buddy system or whatever. You can see it if you watch them long enough. The zoo people feed them leaves and berries. They don't even eat meat.

  We used to have that. Dan and me. We've been partners for ten years. That's a decade. He's like my family. Sometimes I call him Daniel. No one else gets to call him that.

  One time at the zoo, there was this guy walkin around

in a lion's costume. Like that guy from *The Wizard of Oz*. He had this big golden mane. He was like seven feet tall. He was walkin around with a bag of popcorn. As soon as the apes saw him they started beating on their chests and screaming. Their eyes went wild. You could see their teeth like growing in their mouths. They were like *AAAAaaaa! AAAAAaaaa! AAAAaaaa! AAAAaaaa!*...

(DANTLY *seizes the can of Right Guard and starts spraying it wildly around the room, emptying the entire can, still screaming, truly violent.* CASSANDRA *rises, starts to slowly cross to the front door with her suitcase.* DANTLY *eventually stops screaming, sits on the floor, somehow lost.* CASSANDRA *takes another step toward the door.*)

DANTLY: Where you goin? ...Don't go.

(*Suddenly* BURRIS *enters in a panic. He is wet and full of snow. He is holding a snow shovel. He is in shock and his chest is slashed and bloody. He falls down, drops the snow shovel. He stands. He falls down again, gets to his feet, lurches into the bathroom, shuts the door. He can be heard hyperventilating in the bathroom.* CASSANDRA *opens the door.*)

DANTLY: Please don't leave me, Cassandra.

(CASSANDRA *closes the door, turns and crosses back to the chair, sets the suitcase down, sits.* DANTLY *rises off the floor, sits on the edge of the bed. There is an awkward silence.* BURRIS *comes out of the bathroom. He is pressing a towel into his chest.*)

DANTLY: Hey.

BURRIS: Hey.

DANTLY: Zankich just called.

BURRIS: He did?

DANTLY: Yeah. He wants you to call him.

BURRIS: Oh. Right on.

ACT TWO

DANTLY: You gonna call him?

BURRIS: Yeah. Maybe later... Hey, Cassandra. You two getting along well?

(CASSANDRA *doesn't respond.* BURRIS *continues pressing the towel into his chest, in shock.* BURRIS *looks to* DANTLY, *then to* CASSANDRA.)

BURRIS: Aren't you gonna ask me what happened to my chest?

DANTLY: What happened to your chest, Daniel?

BURRIS: There's a fucking bear out there.

DANTLY: Really?

BURRIS: Yeah, man. I'm coming out of that gas station down the street. The guy behind the counter gave me a snow shovel so I could dig the car out. I get about three blocks away and this fucking bear pops out of nowhere. Just like *pop! Pop!* Like someone imagined it or whatever. It totally *am*bushes me, man! I'm like slipping and sliding all over the street, swinging my shovel at him! Snow's swirling in my eyes! Claws are flying! A fucking bear!

DANTLY: Wow. What kind of a bear?

BURRIS: A *bear* bear, man! A big brown fucker! It almost ripped my lungs out!

DANTLY: How'd you get away?

BURRIS: I threw him a box of beef jerky I bought at the gas station. He caught it and headed for the parking lot. I thought he would like go back into the woods and fucking hibernate or whatever, but he crawled on top of the car! It's on top of the fucking car, man! It's out there right now sitting on the hood eating my beef jerky!

DANTLY: *(Winking at* CASSANDRA*)* You should like stand really still.

BURRIS: *What?!*

DANTLY: Nothing.

BURRIS: Where's the gun?!

DANTLY: The gun?

BURRIS: Yeah, the gun. The fucking gun!

DANTLY: Why?

BURRIS: Cause I'm gonna shoot the bear, man!

DANTLY: Oh.

BURRIS: You have the gun, right?

DANTLY: Yeah, I have the gun.

(BURRIS *looks at* CASSANDRA, *who looks away.*)

BURRIS: What's going on, Cassandra?

DANTLY: Hey, Daniel, can I ask you something?

BURRIS: Yeah, sure. What?

DANTLY: What's the deal with all this Mexico stuff?

(BURRIS *looks at* CASSANDRA *again, who looks away, then he looks at* DANTLY.)

BURRIS: What?

DANTLY: Mexico. What's that all about?

(BURRIS *refers to* CASSANDRA, *winks.*)

DANTLY: Cause I like don't have any frequent flier miles, Dan.

BURRIS: Mexico! (*He winks again, nods toward* CASSANDRA.)

DANTLY: Did you hear me? I said I don't have any frequent flier miles.

BURRIS: We're going to Mexico, man! Cancun! The Yucatan Peninsula!

ACT TWO

DANTLY: What did you do with the money, Daniel? Because it's not under the bed. What did you do with it?

BURRIS: Whattaya mean what did I do with it? I made the deal, man.

DANTLY: When?

BURRIS: While you were sleeping.

DANTLY: I don't believe you.

BURRIS: Walt, before I met Cassandra I came back because I forgot my wallet and the phone rang and it was that dude.

DANTLY: Who?

BURRIS: The Fire Man.

DANTLY: The Burning Man.

BURRIS: The Fire Man, the Burning Man, whatever.

DANTLY: The phone rang?

BURRIS: Yeah, the phone rang. You were dead asleep. I met him down by the head shop before I hooked up with Cassandra.

DANTLY: Oh yeah?

BURRIS: Yeah.

DANTLY: That's interesting.

BURRIS: Why is that interesting?

DANTLY: Don't you think that's interesting, Cassandra?

BURRIS: What's so fucking interesting about that?!

DANTLY: What does he look like?

BURRIS: Who?!

DANTLY: The Burning Man. What does he look like? I'm just curious.

(BURRIS *looks at* CASSANDRA, *who looks away.*)

DANTLY: What are you lookin at her for? Does he look like a mosquito?

BURRIS: Does who look like a mosquito?

DANTLY: The Burning Man.

BURRIS: I don't know.

DANTLY: Come on, man.

BURRIS: Come on what? It was dark. It's the middle of the fucking night.

DANTLY: Maybe if you weren't so busy trying to get people to *strum your six-pack* you'd notice the important things! I'll ask you again: Does-he-look-like-a-mosquito!

BURRIS: Why?

DANTLY: It's simple, Daniel: he either *looks* like a mosquito or he *doesn't* look like a mosquito! What's it gonna be?!

(BURRIS *looks at* CASSANDRA *again. She won't look at him.*)

BURRIS: Yeah, *Walter*. I guess he does. I guess he does sorta look like a mosquito.

DANTLY: And he has a lot of nostril hair?

BURRIS: Um, sure. He does, I think. I think his nose is sorta hairy. But it was dark, you know?

DANTLY: Why didn't you take the gun?

BURRIS: Cause I didn't need it, man.

DANTLY: But we always take it when we make the deal.

BURRIS: But we never load it.

DANTLY: But we always take it.

BURRIS: Well, I felt we didn't need it this time.

DANTLY: Really.

ACT TWO

BURRIS: Yeah, really. What the fuck is going on?!

DANTLY: You tell me, Daniel!

BURRIS: Under the circumstances I didn't feel having the gun on my person was necessary. And besides you were all freaked out before so I thought I'd leave it. I figured having it around would make you feel better.

(DANTLY *takes the gun out of the drawer, inserts the clip, considers it, then unloads the clip on* BURRIS. *The shots drive* BURRIS *across the room.* CASSANDRA *is frozen, in shock.*)

(*After a long silence:*)

DANTLY: What were we talkin about, anyway?

CASSANDRA: Cancun and Cazumel. The Yucatan Peninsula.

DANTLY: The Yucatan Peninsula...

(*Pause*)

DANTLY: Is it still snowin?

CASSANDRA: Yeah, it's still coming down.

DANTLY: Do you think it's gonna stop soon?

CASSANDRA: I don't know.

(*The phone rings.* CASSANDRA *lifts her hand to her breast, can feel the wetness coming through her shirt. The phone rings several times, ceases.*)

CASSANDRA: Um, Walt?

DANTLY: Yeah?

CASSANDRA: I'm leaking...I think I'm gonna go.

DANTLY: Okay.

CASSANDRA: ...So bye then.

DANTLY: Bye.

(She opens the door. The snow is horizontal. She exits, closes the door.)

(DANTLY sits at the end of the bed, staring at the bear. He starts to cry. After a moment he rises and crosses to the TV, grabs the plant, stares at himself in the mirror. He puts the plant down, strips completely naked, and then slowly crosses to the front door. He opens the door. The snow is horizontal. He turns back, looks at BURRIS, who is dead, almost perfectly seated against the wall. He crosses to BURRIS with the bear bong, places it in his hand, crosses back to the door. He walks into the snow with the plant, disappearing, leaving the door open.)

(Moments later the phone rings twice.)

(Blackout)

END OF PLAY

www.ingramcontent.com/pod-product-compliance
Lightning Source LLC
Chambersburg PA
CBHW060216050426
42446CB00013B/3088